The Ultimate Soup Maker Recipe Book

Quick, Easy and Delicious Recipes for Every Day incl. Bonus World National Cuisine Soups

Jack Harris

ISBN - 9781679859441

TABLE OF CONTENTS

3

INTRODUCTION

You may only think about soup in those chilly autumn afternoons or those frigid winter nights, but soup is good all year round. Maybe you would like to make the soup more often, but you feel that it is just too involved. After all, you have to chop and sauté and then simmer and boil. Some soups even ask you to take stuff out, blend and then return to simmer some more. Who has time for that? There is a kitchen tool that can help you with that - and no, it is not a slow cooker! It's a soup maker! This device takes all that extra work and utilizes one instrument to complete it in less time than you think (there are even soup makers that have blend modes). These devices are fitted with multiple settings that will have you being able to enjoy those delicious soups you love so much in less than an hour.

If you are a genuine soup enthusiast, owning one of these amazing gadgets may pay off over the long haul. But if you are not, there are several reasons why you should consider one. There are a lot of great benefits. Truth be told, they will undoubtedly positively affect your soup game and diversify your repertoire, by both wiping out irritating little tasks and cutting down the normal planning and execution time needed. We are certain that a soup maker will make you experience some very passionate feelings for cooking soup once you have used one a few times.

While we don't have anything against the traditional stockpot or slow cooker method of cooking soup, the new age of staying up to date with all the new modernized innovations has provoked many into an exploration of this unique and new to the market tool. Here are a few characteristics that soup makers have, that may just convince you to take advantage of all these machines soupy goodness.

SIMPLE AND QUICK

Let's face it. Slicing veggies is one of the most tiresome parts of the whole cooking process. What's more, standing over the pot and stirring isn't that much fun either! All things considered, with a soup maker, both of those things diminish greatly. You are still required to pre-chop your ingredients, but precision isn't a big concern when using a soup maker. The soup maker will do it for you. Simply put everything in and press any of the different buttons to complete different tasks. Then you are free to roam around the house getting stuff done while your soup is being prepared.

LESS CLEAN UP

Regardless of how basic your soup recipe is, it will require at least one cutting board, a blender (on the off chance that you are making a cream soup), a blade, a spoon, and a pot or two. That means a lot of dishes and cleaning up. There must be something that we are overlooking here, but with a soup maker, the fact of the matter is, the main thing that you will have to wash is the container and the blade. Even though you can't just place the soup maker into the dishwasher, a snappy sudsy wash with just a wipe and warm water is all it requires (soup makers with non-stick coatings are the best) which makes clean up easy.

Another significant thing to note here is the way that with a soup maker, it is exceptionally far-fetched to get a dirty counter that is on the off chance that you remember to mix everything with the liquid base before popping the cover on. What's more, regardless of whether you do or don't, simply leave the mess there for an hour with some warm water and cleanser. Once it has soaked for a bit, it will be easily wiped up with just a little scrub of a sponge.

BUDGET-FRIENDLY

Think about all that cash that goes to waste each time you discard excess food! That may seem like a waste, but you know that there is one type of food that is perfect for leftovers! Soup is an extraordinary use for any leftovers to be used in. You won't always use those leftovers in this way, but it makes for a nice way to break up your week and not waste so much food.

Also, you can use this to keep from spending money during those lunch breaks at work. Indeed,owning a soup maker will make things much simpler. You can undoubtedly set up seven days of soup and take it with you for your lunch. This will keep you from eating any of those delicious but dangerously unhealthy foods from chain restaurants, or worse yet, vending machines. You will see your money expenditures drop, and that is a great benefit that anyone would love to take advantage of.

SOUP! IT'S GOOD FOR YOU!

That is the perfect segway into our next benefit that you will be able to reap if you decide to add a soup maker to your kitchen kit. It's an obvious fact that soups are loaded up with those of nutritious and delicious ingredients. And you know precisely what you have put in your own soup maker recipe. This means those dreaded unknown substances, additives, sugar, and other unhealthy ingredients are definitely not included in the creation of your soups. Thus, getting ready soup maker recipes with fresh products will help make sure you get all the vitamins and nutrients you and your family need to remain happy and healthy.

VERSATILE USES

Not only can you choose between having a cream soup or a thick one, but soup makers can also prove to be useful with regards to planning different dishes. Dishes like porridge as well as a wide range of sauces, milkshakes, and smoothies.

This means that you will be able to get more bang for your buck, and that makes a soup maker a good investment. Now that you have an idea of just how awesome soup makers are, let's take a look at how you can use them.

How to Use a Soup Maker?

Using a soup maker is very easy. The first step is always preparation. You can cook meat in the unit, but it works better if it is sautéed or precooked. Other than that, it is totally up to you if you want to sauté before you add the ingredients into the maker. By doing so, though, you may find a deeper and more delicious taste to the finished product. Other than that, there are some tips and tricks that you can use to optimize the performance of your soup maker. These tips and tricks may seem minor but they will have a huge impact on the finished product. Check out all our tips and tricks below that will help you use your soup maker better:

- ⮞ Use water or stock that is already boiling. Though you can use cold tap water often, if you don't use hot water, you may find that your veggies will not come out fully cooked. By starting with hot broth will also allow for the use of other flavorings that using cold liquids may not offer you.

- ⮞ If you intend to use anything frozen, defrost completely before using them. This will keep from overflow issues, as when they thaw, they will create more water which could raise your levels past the fill line on your model.

- ⮞ Ensure all meat that goes into the soup maker is pre-cooked or at least partially cooked. Soup makers don't have long enough settings for cooking your meat to healthy temps. So by recooking your meat, you will be able to make sure you are not going to be sitting down for some chicken noodle soup only to realize your chicken is not cooked through.

- ⮞ Make sure to chop your produce into little pieces, particularly those thicker ones like potatoes. This permits the vegetables to completely cook in the short soup maker cycle. Just like with the meat, the cook cycles on this tool are not long enough to really deal with thick cuts, so chop fine or dice if you want to make sure all your veggies are cooked evenly and fully.

✎ Guarantee the cover is completely shut or fixed. How frustrating would it be if you thought you set your soup to cook, and when you returned, it was not done? Make sure the tops are completely shut or this could happen to you.

✎ Try not to open the cover during cooking. If you do, you may end up splattered with exceptionally hot fluid. That is why in any of the recipes below where you add ingredients after cooking, we made sure to say to only add after the cooking cycle. This will keep you from any unwanted burns.

✎ Some soup makers have a solid pulse setting. This setting may require you to hold the lid down to keep from any hot liquids splashing out of the unit — another safety measure.

✎ Follow your maker's least and most extreme rules. My container has these unmistakably set apart within my machine.

✎ Try not to submerge your soup producer completely in water to clean. Adhere to your guidelines precisely, or you may short out your machine. Most will come with guidelines, but we also cover the basics in the next section, so keep reading.

✎ Adhere to your maker's guidelines for cooking, cleaning, and support. This will ensure that your soup maker stands the test of time and that you will be able to enjoy delicious soups for years to come.

You can use your soup maker, as we have said, for anything from its namesake to smoothies. With a wide range of options, you can see why having one of these tools can only serve to benefit your nightly cooking efforts. But it will be short-lived if you don't take care of it. So now that you have some great tips to use, we should check out some info on the maintenance of this miracle tool.

Maintenance

One of the best things you can do is read your soup maker's instruction guide to ensure you understand all the parts and functions. The most important section is the maintenance. Each model may have varying differences when it comes to the upkeep. With that being said there are quite a few things that are generally universal when it comes to your soup makers maintenance.

You will want to make sure every time you go to clean your soup maker that it is unplugged from its main power source. You should never submerge your soup maker in water, as doing so could cause a short when you plug it in next.

If that is the case, how do you clean it? After all, cleanup is one of the most important parts of the maintenance process. You will want to clean the surfaces instead of the whole unit itself. Here are some steps you can use to clean your soup maker after use:

Clean the inside of the jug:

- Fill the canister up to the fill line with the liquid you are cleaning with.

- Then you will want to shut the lid and press the boil setting.

- When the cycle is done, an alarm will sound and you will be able to dump out the liquid. The cannister should now be perfectly clean.

Cleaning the outside of the sup maker:

- You will want to use a soft, damp cloth to wipe off any food remnants.

᪥ Then you will want to use the same cloth and dip into warm water with mild dish soap. Make sure to ring it out well.

᪥ Go over outside thoroughly. Making sure to get rid of any food remnants you don't get with the first pass.

᪥ When this site is done take a towel and dry thoroughly.

Also, make sure that you unplug your model by grabbing the plug itself and the wire. This will keep potential breaks in the wiring from happening. It will lessen the chance of the unit shorting out which could be dangerous to you and your home.

Maintaining a good maintenance schedule and process will extend the life of your soup maker and protect your form any dangers that may come from using an electrical piece of equipment.

What Do I Need? Preparation

To have everything you need to have before starting, make sure you read the recipe thoroughly. Most often, you will need a cutting board, knife, and ingredients. Having everything prepped properly before starting will save you time and improve the results of your dinner attempts.

Make sure you measure everything out down to the smallest as you are dealing with a limited vessel. One good rule as well is to sauté your meats, so having a skillet and cooking oil handy will be helpful. Also, depending on the unit you are using, you may need a blender near you. Especially if you are looking to craft a cream or thicker soup.

Above all else the first thing you need is the manual and instructions of how your soup maker works. Each one will be a little different and understanding your model will make sure you don't end up with a soup disaster on your hands.

Now that we have given you a tone of great information and tips on how to use it as well as the maintenance it's time to dive into some the most delicious and easy to make soups. We have you covered from the classic to trendy diet recipes for keto and low carb. We are sure you will enjoy these soups no matter what time of year you crave a hot, delicious bowl.

RECIPES

RECIPES

CLASSIC SOUPS

VEGETABLE SOUP

Servings: 4

INGREDIENTS

- 1 sm. onion, sliced
- 2 carrots, chopped
- 2 potatoes, chopped
- 6 oz. swede, diced (175g)
- 6 oz. turnip, diced (175g)
- 3 tomatoes, chopped
- 1 tbsp. parsley, fresh. chopped
- 1½ pints vegetable stock (900ml)
- Salt and pepper to taste

DIRECTIONS

1 Put through the shredding process on the food processor, all the onion, carrots, and potatoes. Place in a soup maker with the swede, turnip, tomatoes, parsley, and stock.

2 Bring to a boil and then let simmer for 30 mins, until vegetables are delicate. Leave to cool for 5 minutes.

3 When done pour out, leaving ½ cup (118mL) in the soup maker, puree the remainder. Then add reminder and puree together for a thicker soup. Serve warm with garnish and sides of your choice.

Nutritional Facts:
Calories: 281
Proteins: 13.3g
Carbs: 58.3g
Fats: 2.4g

MUSHROOM SOUP

Servings: 4

INGREDIENTS

- 2 cups water (500mL)
- 1 clove garlic, chopped
- 7 oz. cream (250 ml)
- 9 oz. mushrooms (250 g)
- 1 sm. potato, chopped
- 2 bouillon cubes
- Pinch of nutmeg

DIRECTIONS

1 Put everything in the soup maker and choose the correct setting.

2 When done, serve with your favorite garnishes.

Nutritional Facts:

Calories: 257

Proteins: 8g

Carbs: 63.5g

Fats: 1g

HAM & SPLIT PEA SOUP

Servings: 4

INGREDIENTS

- 9 oz. split peas, soaked and drained (250g)
- 7 oz. lean ham (200g) – 1 oz. for garnish
- 1 onion, diced
- 1 carrot, diced
- 1 celery stick, diced
- 2 cloves garlic, minced
- 1 tsp. thyme
- 4 cups water (1L)
- 2½ bouillon cubes
- Season to taste

DIRECTIONS

1 Soak peas overnight and then drain and rinse. Heat oil in a skillet and sauté all the veg on medium to low for around 10 mins or until the onions are slightly tender.

2 In a skillet heat oil and sauté ham. Set aside some for garnishing but add the rest to the soup maker.

3 Move everything else into the soup maker and set it to smooth. If not to the full line, add some water to reach it.

4 Cook until done and serve topped with ham.

Nutritional Facts:

Calories: 95

Proteins: 10.7g

Carbs: 9.3g

Fats: 1.9g

TOMATO SOUP

Servings: 4

INGREDIENTS

- 1 onion, diced
- 1 bay leaf
- 4 cloves garlic, chopped
- 1 tbsp. sugar
- 1½ tsp. Cajun seasoning
- 1 tsp. salt
- 1 lrg. carrot, diced
- 2 sweet potatoes, cubed
- 28 oz. whole tomatoes (800g)
- 4 cups vegetable stock (1liter)
- Salt and pepper to taste
- Basil, parsley or thyme leaves

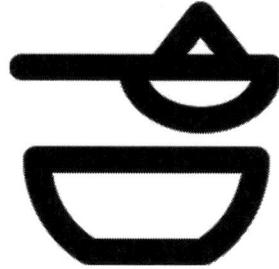

DIRECTIONS

1 Add all the ingredients into the soup maker, using the back of a spoon press everything down.

2 Pour in the stock to the fill-up line. Select smooth and let it run until the soup is mixed. Check the flavoring and adjust as needed.

Nutritional Facts:

Calories: 144

Proteins: 5g

Carbs: 33.1g

Fats: 1g

CHICKEN SOUP

Servings: 4

INGREDIENTS

- 4 oz. carrots, chopped (120g)
- 11 oz. chicken breast, cubed (300g)
- 2 oz. onions, chopped (60 g)
- 4 oz. sweet corn, drained (120g)
- 2½ cups chicken stock (600mL)
- pepper and salt to taste
- 1 tbsp. parsley, fresh, chopped
- 6 sprigs thyme

DIRECTIONS

1 In a skillet heat oil and sauté chicken until browned on all sides. Add it into the soup maker.

2 Prep all fresh ingredients. Then place them into the soup maker, close the cover and press the thick soup setting.

3 At the point when the soup is ready, serve garnished with parsley.

Nutritional Facts:

Calories: 183

Proteins: 17.6g

Carbs: 12.5g

Fats: 7.4g

PUMPKIN SOUP

Servings: 2

INGREDIENTS

- 1 lb. pumpkin, cubed (500g)
- 3 cloves garlic, chopped
- 1 sm. onion, diced
- 2 tsp. herb mix
- salt and pepper to taste

DIRECTIONS

1   Prep all the ingredients; season with salt, pepper, and herbs. Pour in a cup of cold water (200mL).

2   Close top of the soup maker and set it to a thick soup. When cooked, check to ensure there is sufficient fluid to make into a smooth soup and utilize the mix feature.

3   Spoon in a tablespoon of your preferred half and a half and serve warm.

Nutritional Facts:

Calories: 39

Proteins: 1g

Carbs: 7g

Fats: 1g

MINESTRONE

Servings: 6

INGREDIENTS

- 6 lrg. carrots, chopped
- 3 med. mushrooms, sliced
- 1 med. onion, chopped
- 1 bunch Brussel sprouts, quartered
- ½ bag baby spinach
- 3 tomatoes, diced
- 1 can stewed tomatoes
- 1 can kidney beans
- 2 oz. peas, frozen (50g)
- 2 tsps. garlic puree
- 2 tsps. tomato puree
- 4 oz. pasta (100g)
- 5 oz. water (150mL)
- 1 tsp. oregano
- 1 tsp. rosemary
- 3 bay leaves
- Salt and pepper to taste

DIRECTIONS

1 Prep the carrots, onions, mushrooms, and tomatoes; add them to your soup maker. Then include the sprouts, spinach, stewed tomatoes, kidney beans, peas, pasta, and flavoring.

2 Pour the water over and cook for 25 minutes on the thick soup. Serve with some fresh crusty bread.

Nutritional Facts:

Calories: 119

Proteins: 4g

Carbs: 25g

Fats: 0g

TURKEY SOUP

Servings: 4

INGREDIENTS

- 1 med. onion, diced
- 2 lrg. potatoes, diced
- 8 med. carrots, diced
- 1/3 head of cauliflower, diced
- 2 tbsp. Greek yogurt
- 2 tbsp. cream cheese
- 1 tsp. garlic puree
- 7 oz. shredded turkey (200g)
- 3 oz. water (100mL)
- 1 tsp. thyme
- Salt and pepper to taste

DIRECTIONS

1 Prep all the ingredients and then add them to the soup maker. Add the water, salt, and pepper.

2 Cook for 25 minutes in the soup maker. Drain most of the water from the soup maker and add the flavoring, Greek yogurt, cheese, and turkey. Mix and serve.

Nutritional Facts:

Calories: 207

Proteins: 13g

Carbs: 29g

Fats: 5g

CHICKEN NOODLE SOUP

Servings: 8

INGREDIENTS

- 2 tbsp. butter
- 1 lrg. onion, chopped
- 2med. carrots, sliced
- 2 stalks celery, sliced
- Salt and pepper to taste
- 1 tbsp. thyme, fresh, chopped
- 1 tbsp. parsley, fresh, chopped
- 1 tbsp. oregano, fresh, chopped
- 4 cups chicken broth (940mL)
- 2 lbs. chicken breasts, skin on, bone-in (907g)
- 4 cups water (1000mL)
- 5 oz. egg noodles (142g)

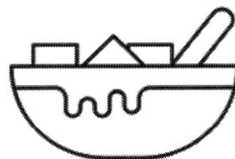

DIRECTIONS

1 Sauté the onions, carrots, and celery in butter until slightly tender; add into soup maker. In the same skillet toss in the chicken and cook until it is browned. Season with salt and pepper, include the thyme, parsley, oregano, and mix.

2 Pour in the chicken broth. Include the chicken pieces, pasta, and 4 cups of water.

3 Close the top and set the soup maker to a thick soup setting. When done, remove chicken and shred with two forks. Add the chicken back; taste for flavoring and adjust accordingly.

Nutritional Facts:

Calories: 374

Proteins: 26g

Carbs: 18g

Fats: 21g

CABBAGE SOUP

Servings: 3

INGREDIENTS

- ½ lrg. head of cabbage, chopped
- ¼ lrg. zucchini
- 3 med. carrots, diced
- 1 tsp. chives, chopped
- 1 tsp. parsley, chopped
- 1½ cups water(300 mL)
- Salt and pepper to taste

DIRECTIONS

1 Prep all your vegetables and place them in the soup maker.

2 Set to cook. Then serve with some crusty bread.

Nutritional Facts:

Calories: 65

Proteins: 2g

Carbs: 15g

Fats: 0g

LENTIL SOUP

Servings: 6

INGREDIENTS

- 7 oz. split red lentils, rinsed and soaked (200g)
- 4 cups vegetable stock (1L)
- 7 oz. potatoes, cubed (200g)
- 1 tsp. pepper
- 1 sm. onion, chopped

DIRECTIONS

1   Sauté onions in skillet until just softened. Add all ingredients into the soup maker

2   Select the thick setting and cook. Serve with some fresh bread.

Nutritional Facts:

Calories: 154

Proteins: 29g

Carbs: 9g

Fats: 1g

FRENCH ONION SOUP

Servings: 4

INGREDIENTS

- 5 Large Onion stripped
- 3 Large Carrots stripped
- 5 Large Celery Sticks
- 2 tbsp Greek Yogurt
- 250 ml Water
- 2 tsp Chives
- 1 tsp Mixed Herbs
- 1 tsp Thyme
- Salt and Pepper

DIRECTIONS

1 Prep all the ingredients; place them in the soup maker

2 Cook on the thick soup setting for 25 minutes. Pour into ramekins and top with dry crusty bread and cheese. Broil in the oven until the cheese is melted and lightly brown. Serve.

Nutritional Facts:

Calories: 94

Proteins: 3g

Carbs: 19g

Fats: 0g

CREAM SOUPS

POTATO AND LEEK

Servings: 6

INGREDIENTS

- 1 lb. potatoes, chopped (500g)
- ½ lb. leeks, chopped (200g)
- 4 oz. onion, chopped (100g)
- Salt and pepper to taste
- 3oz. cream (100ml)
- 3 cups of boiling water (700ml)
- 1 bouillon cube, smashed

DIRECTIONS

1 Put all the ingredients into the soup maker. Set to the smooth setting. Cook for 21 minutes.

2 Serve with crisp bread and parsley.

Nutritional Facts:

Calories: 93

Proteins: 2.5g

Carbs: 21.2

Fats: 0g

TOMATO AND ROSEMARY

Servings: 5

INGREDIENTS

- 1 stalk celery, chopped
- 3oz. smoked bacon, chopped fine (75g)
- 1 shallot, chopped
- 1 med. carrot, chopped
- 14 oz. tomatoes, chopped (400g)
- 1 can stewed tomatoes
- 2 cloves garlic, chopped
- 1oz. white wine (30mL)
- 1½ cups vegetable stock (400mL)
- 1 tbsp. rosemary, fresh, chopped
- 1 tbsp. thyme, fresh, chopped
- 1 tsp. maple syrup
- Salt and pepper to taste
- 1 tbsp. parsley, fresh, chopped
- ½ cup of cream (125mL)

DIRECTIONS

1 Prep veggies and cook bacon. Put all the ingredients in the soup maker. Season. Pick the creamed soup setting.

2 When cooked, open soup maker and mix in parsley and cream. Season to taste.

3 Serve warm garnished with extra cream and parsley.

Nutritional Facts:

Calories: 87

Proteins: 3.7g

Carbs: 9.4g

Fats: 5g

CREAM OF EGGPLANT

Servings: 6

INGREDIENTS

- 1 lb. eggplant, cubed (500g)
- ½ lb. butter beans (200g)
- 1 vegetable stock pot
- 1 herb flavor stock pot
- ½ cup fresh cream (150mL)
- 700ml Boiling Water

DIRECTIONS

1 Add all the ingredients to the pot and cook on the cream soup setting for 30 minutes.

2 Serve topped with a garnish of your choice.

Nutritional Facts:

Calories: 162

Proteins: 11.1g

Carbs: 3g

Fats: 11.6g

CREAM OF BROCCOLI

Servings: 4

INGREDIENTS

- 1/5 med. zucchini, chopped
- 1 med. head of broccoli, chopped
- 1 sm. onion, chopped
- 1 tsp. oregano
- 1 tsp. thyme
- 2 cups water (468mL)
- 2 tbsp. Greek yogurt
- Salt and pepper to taste

DIRECTIONS

1 Prep your vegetables and add them to your soup maker. Cover with the water and add the seasoning. Cook for 25 minutes on the cream setting.

2 Then mix in the Greek Yogurt and blend it in well. Modify with additional water if necessary. Serve warm topped with a topping of your choice.

Nutritional Facts:

Calories: 70

Proteins: 5g

Carbs: 13g

Fats: 0g

CREAMY CAULIFLOWER

Servings: 6

INGREDIENTS

- 1 med. head of cauliflower
- 1 lrg. onion, chopped
- 1 sm. butternut squash, chopped
- 1 lrg. bell pepper, yellow
- 4 tbsp. Greek yogurt
- 1 cup water (250mL)
- 1 tsp. herb mix
- 1 tsp. parsley
- Salt and pepper to taste

DIRECTIONS

1 Prep all vegetables and add them to the soup maker. Pour in water and seasoning.

2 Put your soup maker on for 25 minutes on the cook and mix setting. When cooked include your Greek yogurt, mix again and serve.

Nutritional Facts:

Calories: 85

Proteins: 3g

Carbs: 19g

Fats: 0g

CREAM OF PARSNIP

Servings: 4

INGREDIENTS

- 2 sweet potatoes, chopped
- 1 lrg. onion
- 4 med. parsnips
- 2 lrg. carrots
- 1 tsp. garlic puree
- 3 oz. water (100mL)
- 1 tsp. thyme
- Salt and pepper to taste

DIRECTIONS

1 Clean and cut the sweet potatoes, onion, parsnip, and carrots and put them in the soup maker. Include the garlic puree, water, and seasonings.

2 Cook for 25 minutes on the cook and mix setting. Serve topped with your choice of garnishes.

Nutritional Facts:

Calories: 197

Proteins: 3g

Carbs: 46g

Fats: 0g

CREAMY SPICED CARROT SOUP

Servings: 4

INGREDIENTS

- 12 lrg. carrots, chopped
- 1 lrg. onion. chopped
- 1 bell pepper, red, chopped
- 2 tsps. garlic puree
- 1 tbsp. honey
- 1 can coconut milk
- 3 cups water (100mL)
- 1 tsp. cinnamon
- 1 tsp. turmeric
- ¼" ginger, fresh, (1cm)
- 2 tbsp. coriander
- Salt and pepper to taste

DIRECTIONS

1 Cut and place all vegetables into your soup maker. Then add in the ginger, garlic, and other seasonings.

2 Add the coconut milk and water; Set for the cook and mix setting for 25 minutes. Serve topped with your favorite garnishes.

Nutritional Facts:

Calories: 351

Proteins: 5g

Carbs: 34g

Fats: 24g

BUTTERNUT AND APPLE SOUP

Servings: 4

INGREDIENTS

- 3 med. apples, chopped
- 1 sm. onion, diced
- 7 oz. butternut squash, chopped (200g)
- 2 oz. pumpkin, chopped (50g)
- 1 tsp. cumin
- 2 tsps. coriander
- 1 tsp. allspice
- 1 tsp. paprika
- 1 tsp. ginger puree
- 2 tsps. garlic puree
- 2 tbsp. Greek yogurt
- 3 oz. water (100mL)
- Salt and pepper to taste

DIRECTIONS

1 Prep all the produce and place them in the soup maker. Pour in the water and seasoning.

2 Cook on the cook and mix setting for 25 minutes. Then when done add in the yogurt and blend well. Serve warm with a dollop of Greek yogurt.

Nutritional Facts:

Calories: 124

Proteins: 2g

Carbs: 30g

Fats: 0g

CREAM OF CELERY

Servings: 4

INGREDIENTS

- ◆ 6 stalks celery, chopped
- ◆ 1 lrg. onion, diced
- ◆ 4 lrg. carrots, chopped
- ◆ 1 cup water (250mL)
- ◆ 2 tbsp. cream cheese
- ◆ 1 tsp. herb mix
- ◆ 1 tsp. chives, fresh, chopped
- ◆ Salt and pepper to taste

DIRECTIONS

1 Chop your celery, onion, and carrots. Place in the soup maker. Add the water and seasoning; set for the cook and mix setting. Cook for 25 minutes.

2 Then add the cheese, mix again and serve.

Nutritional Facts:

Calories: 76

Proteins: 2g

Carbs: 10g

Fats: 3g

CREAMY GREEK GREENS SOUP

Servings: 2

INGREDIENTS

- 3.5 oz. broccoli, chopped (100g)
- ½ med. zucchini
- 3.5 oz. savoy cabbage (100g)
- 4 asparagus spears, chopped
- Bunch of baby spinach. fresh
- 1 sm. bag frozen peas
- 2 tsps. garlic puree
- Vegetable bouillon cube
- 1 tbsp. thyme, fresh, chopped
- 1 tbsp. mint, fresh, chopped
- 1 tsp. parsley, fresh, chopped
- Salt and pepper to taste
- 1 tsp. Greek yogurt

DIRECTIONS

1 Clean and prep all your fresh ingredients. Place all the vegetables into the base of the soup maker. Add the water, bouillon, and seasonings (except the garlic puree).

2 Close the top of your soup maker; cook for 28 minutes. When cooked, include the garlic puree and blend for a few minutes. Serve topped with Greek yogurt.

Nutritional Facts:

Calories: 58
Proteins: 4g
Carbs: 11g
Fats: 0g

VEGETABLE CURRY

Servings: 4

INGREDIENTS

- 1 med. leek, chopped
- 3 lrg. carrots, chopped
- 1 sm. zucchini
- 7 oz. pumpkin, diced (200g)
- 1 sm. bell pepper, red, chopped
- 1 can coconut milk
- 1 tsp. Thai curry paste
- 1 tsp. garlic puree
- 1 tsp. mustard
- 1 tsp. coriander
- 2 tsp. paprika
- 1 tsp. allspice
- 3 oz. water (100mL)
- Salt and pepper to taste

DIRECTIONS

1 Clean and chop your vegetables. Place your vegetables into the soup maker; add in your water and coconut milk. Sprinkle in your herbs and seasonings.

2 Cook on the thick soup setting for 25 minutes. Serve it with dry bread.

Nutritional Facts:

Calories: 302

Proteins: 4g

Carbs: 21g

Fats: 24g

BROCCOLI GRATIN

Servings: 4

INGREDIENTS

- 2 lrg. carrots, chopped
- 1 sm. head of broccoli, chopped
- 3 oz. zucchini, chopped (75g)
- ½ lrg. onion, chopped
- 1/3 lrg. head of cauliflower, chopped
- 1 tsp. garlic puree
- 2 oz. cheese, shredded (50g)
- 1 tbsp. cream cheese
- 4 tbsp. coconut milk
- 2 tsp. parsley, fresh, chopped
- 3oz. water (100mL)
- Salt and pepper to taste

DIRECTIONS

1 Clean and cut all the vegetables and herbs. Place all the vegetables into the soup maker. Cook for 25 minutes.

2 When they are cooked, drain the maker and add to the vegetables the cheddar, coconut milk, garlic, parsley alongside the salt and pepper. Mix until smooth. Then serve.

Nutritional Facts:

Calories: 169

Proteins: 8g

Carbs: 16g

Fats: 9g

SOUPS WITH MEAT

HUNGARIAN GOULASH

Servings: 5

INGREDIENTS

- 2 tbsp. olive oil
- 2 onions, diced
- 3 cloves garlic, chopped
- 1 tsp. caraway seeds
- 1 tsp. salt
- 2 lbs. stewing meat, cubed (950g)
- 2 tbsp. sweet Hungarian paprika
- ½ tsp. cayenne pepper
- 2 cups beef stock (500ml)
- 14 oz. tomatoes, chopped (400g)
- 3 carrots, chopped
- 3 potatoes, cubed
- 2 bell peppers, red, cut
- Salt and pepper to taste
- Sour cream

DIRECTIONS

1. Heat the oil in a skillet and cook the onions and peppers for 5 minutes; add in the garlic and caraway seeds. Brown the meat. Add all of that plus the paprika, carrots, and potatoes into the soup maker. Pour in the stock and top with the tomatoes.

2. Set to cook on the thick setting; cook for 30 minutes. Check seasonings and adjust as needed. Serve with a dollop of sour cream.

Nutritional Facts:

Calories: 473

Proteins: 44g

Carbs: 32g

Fats: 19g

GREEK LEMON CHICKEN SOUP

Servings: 6

INGREDIENTS

- 1 tbsp. olive oil
- ¾ cupcarrot, diced (170g)
- ½ cup onion, chopped(113g)
- 2 tsps. garlic, minced
- ¾ tsp. red pepper flakes
- 6 cups chicken stock (1L)
- ½ cup orzo (113g)
- 3 huge eggs
- ¼ cup lemon juice, fresh (59mL)
- 3 cups rotisserie chicken, shredded (680g)
- 3 cups baby spinach, chopped (680g)
- ¼ tsp. salt
- ½ tsp. pepper
- 3 tbsp. dill, fresh, chopped

DIRECTIONS

1 Prep all the vegetables and place all the ingredients in the soup maker. Add in the orzo and cook on a thick soup setting for 25 minutes.

2 While it cooks, whisk eggs and lemon together. Then open the pot, take some of the stock and slowly add it into the egg mixture. Once combined, add in batches and mix.

3 Then serve garnished with dill.

Nutritional Facts:

Calories: 261

Proteins: 32g

Carbs: 16g

Fats: 8g

LASAGNA SOUP

Servings: 8

INGREDIENTS

- 1 lb. lean ground beef (454g)
- 8 oz. mushrooms, quartered (227g)
- 1 cup onion, chopped (227g)
- 1 cup bell pepper, red, chopped (227g)
- 2 cloves garlic, minced
- 4 cups chicken stock (946mL)
- 1 can crushed tomatoes
- 6-oz. tomato paste (170g)
- 2 tsps. dried oregano
- 1 tsp. salt
- ¼ tsp. pepper
- 8 oz. lasagna noodles, broken (227g)
- ¼ cup cream (59mL)
- 4 oz. mozzarella, shredded (113g)
- ½ cup basil, fresh, chopped (113g)

DIRECTIONS

1 Cook hamburger in a huge nonstick skillet over a medium heat until sautéed and crumbled around 5 minutes. Move to soup maker. Include mushrooms, onion, ringer pepper, and garlic, and mix to consolidate. Include stock, tomatoes, tomato paste, oregano, salt, and pepper. Cook on thick soup for 25 minutes.

2 Cook lasagna noodles until al dente. When the soup is done, pour into the stockpot and add in the noodles and cream. Serve topped with mozzarella and basil.

Nutritional Facts:

Calories: 276

Proteins: 23g

Carbs: 33g

Fats: 8g

BEEF AND NOODLE SOUP VIETNAMESE-STYLE

Servings: 4

INGREDIENTS

- 3 whole star anise
- 1 cinnamon stick
- 2 med. onions
- 3 tbsp. ginger, fresh, minced
- ½ lb. bone-in short ribs, beef (227g)
- 1 cup water (237mL)
- 4 cups beef stock (946mL)
- ¼ tsp. salt
- 2¼ tsps. fish sauce
- 2 tsps. hoisin sauce
- 4 oz. brown rice vermicelli (113g)
- 4 oz top sirloin steak, sliced (113g)
- 2 cups bean sprouts, fresh (454g)
- 1 cup basil, fresh, chopped (227g)
- ½ cup mint, fresh, chopped (113g)
- 1 lime, cut into 4 wedges
- Fresno chile, sliced thin

DIRECTIONS

1 Add in all ingredients from the star anise to the short ribs into a slow cooker. Cook on high for about 2 hours. Remove and strain the broth. Place strained broth in the soup maker. Shred ribs off of bone and place in the soup maker. Add in the fish sauce, hoisin, and vermicelli. Cook on thick soup for 20 minutes.

2 While it is cooking, salt and pepper your sirloin and grill in a hot skillet, then slice thin. In bowls, pour soup and top with sirloin, sprouts, basil, and mint. Serve garnished with a lime and Fresno chili.

Nutritional Facts:

Calories: 337

Proteins: 26g

Carbs: 38g

Fats: 9g

ITALIAN WEDDING SOUP

Servings: 6

INGREDIENTS

- 12 oz. Italian sausage (340g)
- 1 tbsp. olive oil
- ¾ cup onion, chopped (113g)
- ¾ cup carrot, chopped (170g)
- 2 cloves garlic, minced
- 3 cups chicken stock (710mL)
- 2 cups water (473mL)
- 5 cups baby spinach (1kg)
- ¼ cup dill, fresh. chopped (57g)
- 2 tsps. lemon juice, fresh
- ½ tsp. salt
- ½ tsp. pepper
- 4 tbsp. Parmesan, grated

DIRECTIONS

1 Roll sausage into small meatballs. Heat the olive oil in a skillet over medium to high heat. Add in the meatballs; cook until browned on all sides. Remove meatballs from skillet.

2 Add onion, carrot, minced garlic, chicken stock, spinach, dill, lemon juice, salt, pepper, and water; Cook on thick soup for 25 minutes.

3 Place several meatballs into individual bowls. Pour soup from the maker over each and top with grated parmesan.

Nutritional Facts:

Calories: 234

Proteins: 14g

Carbs: 11g

Fats: 15g

GARLICKY LENTIL SOUP

Servings: 6

INGREDIENTS

- 1 tbsp. grapeseed oil
- 1 sm. onion, sliced
- 2 bell peppers, green, chopped
- 1 serrano chile, chopped fine
- 6 cups of chicken juices, isolated
- 25 cloves black garlic
- 1 tbsp. red pepper flakes
- 3 med. tomatoes, chopped
- 1 ¾ cups dried black lentils
- 12 oz. chorizo (340g)
- 12 cloves garlic, finely chopped
- 12 oz. mushrooms, cut thin (340g)
- 2 bay leaves
- 2 tbsp. hot Hungarian paprika
- 2 tbsp. apple cider vinegar
- 2 tsps. pepper
- 1 cup red peppers, cut (227g)
- Sour cream, green onions, and fresh cilantro

DIRECTIONS

1. Sauté the onions, peppers, and chili. Cook until tender and then add into the soup maker. Add in the broth, black garlic, and chilis. Then add in the rest of the ingredients. Brown sausage in skillet and add into the maker. Cook on a thick soup setting for 25 minutes.

2 When finished adding into a stockpot. Add in vinegar and salt, season to taste with pepper. Serve garnished with sour cream, green onions, and cilantro

Nutritional Facts:

Calories: 844
Proteins: 73gg
Carbs: 100g
Fats: 27.5g

CHICKEN & KALE

Servings: 4

INGREDIENTS

- 1 tbsp. olive oil
- 1 cup onion, chopped(227g)
- ½ cup carrot, chopped (113g)
- ½ tsp. red pepper flake
- 3/8 tsp. salt
- 3 cloves garlic, minced
- 2 thyme sprigs
- 4 cups chicken stock (946mL)
- 1 can chickpeas, drained and rinsed
- 2 cups kale, chopped (453g)
- 8 oz. rotisserie chicken, shredded (227g)
- 1 tsp. soy sauce

DIRECTIONS

1 Add all ingredients into the soup maker except shredded chicken; cook on thick soup setting for 25 minutes. Then add in the chicken and serve.

Nutritional Facts:

Calories: 264

Proteins: 26g

Carbs: 23g

Fats: 8.4g

BACON, CHICKEN POTATO SOUP

Servings: 6

INGREDIENTS

- 4 bacon slices, diced
- ½ lbs. bone-in chicken thighs (227g)
- 2 cups leek, chopped (454g)
- 1 cup carrot, chopped (227g)
- 1 cup celery, chopped (227g)
- 4 cups chicken stock (946mL)
- ¾ tsp. salt
- ½ tsp. pepper
- 5 thyme sprigs
- 12 oz. baby potatoes (340g)
- 2 cups baby spinach, chopped (454g)

DIRECTIONS

1 Cook bacon in a huge skillet over medium-high until fresh. Remove bacon from skillet and drain on paper towels. Cook chicken thighs in leftover bacon drippings until browned.

2 Add all ingredients except spinach, not the soup maker. Pour broth and seasonings into the maker. Cook on the cream and mix setting for 25 minutes.

3 When done then add in the spinach and blend until spinach wilts. Serve topped with shredded cheese.

Nutritional Facts:

Calories: 174

Proteins: 19g

Carbs: 14g

Fats: 4.3g

SOUPS WITH FISH

CIOPPINO

Servings: 4

INGREDIENTS

- ♦ 2 tbsp. extra-virgin olive oil
- ♦ ½ cups onion, chopped (113g)
- ♦ ½ cups fennel, chopped (113g)
- ♦ 10 cloves garlic, chopped
- ♦ 1 cup dry white wine (237mL)
- ♦ 2 tsps. tomato paste
- ♦ ½ cup of water (118mL)
- ♦ 2 tbsp. oregano, fresh, chopped
- ♦ 2 tbsp. thyme, fresh, chopped
- ♦ ¾ tsp. red pepper flakes
- ♦ 3/8 tsp. salt
- ♦ ½ lb. tomatoes, chopped (227g)
- ♦ Several lemon skin strips
- ♦ 2 bay leaves
- ♦ 1 crate cherry tomatoes, chopped
- ♦ ¾ lb. cod, cut into 2-inch pieces (340g)
- ♦ ½ lb. scallops (113g)
- ♦ ½ lb. shrimp (113g)
- ♦ 1 tbsp. lemon juice, fresh
- ♦ ¼ cup basil, fresh, chopped (57g)

DIRECTIONS

1 Heat oil in a skillet and onion, fennel, and garlic; cook until delicate. Add wine and tomato paste to skillet, mix well. Cook for 2 minutes. Put in the soup maker.

2 Include 1/2 cup water and all the ingredients except fish, lemon juice and basil. Cool on thick soup setting for 20 minutes.

3 When done strain out lemon peel and bay leaf. Add in remaining ingredients (except basil) and cook for another 10 minutes. Reveal; dispose of lemon skin and straight leaves. Serve garnished with basil.

Nutritional Facts:

Calories: 338

Proteins: 34g

Carbs: 29g

Fats: 8.7g

COCONUT SHRIMP SOUP

Servings: 6

INGREDIENTS

- 1 lb. shrimp (454g)
- 1 tbsp. ginger, fresh, grated
- 4 cloves garlic, minced
- 2 tsps. olive oil
- 4 cups of vegetable broth (946mL)
- 1 can coconut milk
- 2½ tbsp. fish sauce
- 1 tbsp. light brown sugar
- 1 tbsp. lime juice, fresh
- 2 tsps. red curry paste
- 2 cups mushrooms, sliced (454g)
- 1 med. bell pepper, red, chopped
- ¼ cup basil, fresh, chopped (57g)
- ¼ cup cilantro, fresh, chopped (57g)
- ¼ cup green onions, chopped (57g)
- 1 Thai chile pepper, minced

DIRECTIONS

1 Prep all the ingredients and place all in the soup maker except the shrimp, basil, cilantro, green onions, and chili. Cook for 15 minutes.

2 Add in the shrimp and cook for another 10 minutes. Serve garnished with basil, cilantro, and chilis.

Nutritional Facts:

Calories: 554

Proteins: 6.3g

Carbs: 46g

Fats: 41.4g

HOT & SOUR SHRIMP SOUP

Servings: 4

INGREDIENTS

- 2 lemongrass stalks
- 6 cups chicken broth (1L)
- 1 serrano chiles, chopped
- 1 shallot, chopped
- 2 pieces ginger, fresh, squashed
- 1 sm. zucchini, chopped
- 4 mushrooms, quartered
- 1 red jalapeño chile, chopped fine
- ¾ lb. sm. shrimp (340g)
- 1 tbsp. fish sauce
- 1 tbsp. white vinegar
- ¼ cup cilantro, fresh (57g)
- 2 tbsp. dill, fresh, chopped

DIRECTIONS

1 Trim green tips from lemongrass and strip off the external layer. Crush stalks and tie together. Put in a stockpot, include broth, serrano chile, shallot, and ginger, and heat until boiling over high warmth. Diminish warmth to a medium heat and simmer for 10 minutes.

2 While you are creating the broth, add the remaining ingredients (except shrimp, fish sauce, vinegar, cilantro, and dill) into the soup maker. Remove lemongrass from broth and add it to the soup maker as well. Cook for 15 minutes.

3 Add in shrimp and cook for another 5 minutes. Then remove soup and mix in fish sauce, vinegar, cilantro, and dill. Serve.

Nutritional Facts:

Calories: 160

Proteins: 25g

Carbs: 8.4g

Fats: 3.7g

SPICY CLAM AND WHITE BEAN SOUP

Servings: 8

INGREDIENTS

- 2 tbsp. olive oil
- 6 oz. dried aged chorizo, chopped (170g)
- 1 med. onion, chopped
- 1 lrg. bell pepper, red, chopped
- 2 tbsp. oregano, fresh, chopped
- 6 cloves garlic, chopped
- 1 lrg. potato, cubed
- 1 tsp. salt
- 1 tsp. paprika
- ½ tsp. red pepper flakes
- 4 cups chicken broth (946mL)
- 2 cans cannellini beans, rinsed and drained
- 40 littleneck clams, cleaned
- 2 tsps. lemon juice, fresh
- 1/3 cup scallions, chopped (71g)
- 3 cups white wine (709mL)

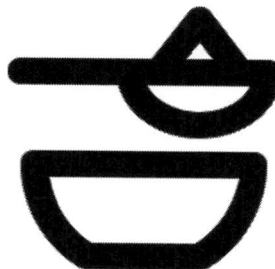

DIRECTIONS

1 Heat chorizo in a skillet and sauté onions, garlic, and peppers. Then add it into the soup maker along with the remaining ingredients, except the clams, lemon, and scallions. Cook for 20 minutes.

2 While that cooks in a stockpot heat wine. Place clams in the pot and steam until open. Place clams in bowls and ladle the soup over the top. Serve with a squeeze of lemon juice and garnished with scallions.

Nutritional Facts:

Calories: 134

Proteins: 4.5g

Carbs: 17.1g

Fats: 5.9g

SEAFOOD GUMBO

Servings: 6

INGREDIENTS

- ½ lb. lump crabmeat (227g)
- 1½ lbs. med. shrimp (with heads) (680g)
- 6 tbsp. oil
- 1 lb. okra, frozen (454g)
- ½ tsp. salt
- ½ lb. andouille sausage, chopped (454g)
- 2 tbsp. all-purpose flour
- 2 cups onion, chopped fine(454g)
- ½ cup celery, chopped fine (113g)
- ½ cup bell pepper, green, choppedfine (113g)
- 4 cloves garlic, minced
- ½ cup green onions, chopped(113g)
- 1 sm. can tomato paste
- 3 bay leaves
- 1 tsp. thyme. Fresh, chopped
- 2 tsps. salt
- 1 tsp. hot sauce
- ¼ tsp. cayenne pepper
- ½ tsp. pepper
- 1 tbsp. Worcestershire sauce
- 1 can entire tomatoes
- 24 oysters
- ¼ cup parsley, fresh, chopped (57g)
- Hot cooked long-grain rice

DIRECTIONS

1 Fill a stockpot with water and shells from shrimp. Bring to a boil and allow to simmer for an hour. In a large skillet, sauté andouille and set aside. Add in the flour and whisk until mixture is a light chocolate color. Add in the onion, bell pepper, and celery. Cook for a few minutes and then add in the garlic. Once that has sautéed a few minutes add in the tomato paste.

2 Add all ingredients except the fish into the soup maker and now take stock and begin to ladle in the shrimp broth into the skillet until the roux is dissolved into the broth. Now add it to the soup maker. Cook on the thick setting for 20 minutes.

3 Then add in the fish and cook for another 5 minutes or until shrimp are pink. When done add sausage back in. Serve over rice.

Nutritional Facts:

Calories: 389

Proteins: 26.2g

Carbs: 21.8g

Fats: 23.7g

CORN CHOWDER WITH SHRIMP

Servings: 4

INGREDIENTS

- 6 slices bacon, chopped
- 1 cup onion, chopped (227g)
- ½ cup celery, chopped (113g)
- 1 tsp. thyme, fresh, chopped
- 1 clove garlic, minced
- 4 cups frozen corn, defrosted (907g)
- 2 cups chicken stock (473mL)
- ¾ lb. med. shrimp (340g)
- 1/3 cup cream (78mL)
- ¼ tsp. pepper
- 1/8 tsp. salt

DIRECTIONS

1 Place all ingredients except the shrimp and cream into the soup maker. Cook on a thick soup setting for 20 minutes. Then remove two cups and blend. Replace blended soup; add in cream and shrimp into the soup maker and cook for another 10 minutes.

2 In a large skillet cook bacon until crisp. Then serve the soup with it garnishing the top.

Nutritional Facts:

Calories: 294

Proteins: 26.8g

Carbs: 34.8g

Fats: 7g

BOUILLABAISSE

Servings: 6

INGREDIENTS

- 8 cups pumpkin (2kg)
- 3 tbsp. olive oil
- 1 lrg. fennel bulb, chopped
- 2 leeks, chopped
- 10 cloves garlic, chopped
- ¾ cups white wine (177mL)
- 4 cups chicken broth (946mL)
- ½ tsp. turmeric
- 1 dried bay leaf
- ½ tsp. salt
- ½ tsp. pepper
- 3½ cups tomatoes, chopped (794g)
- ¾ lb. halibut, cut into 1-inch pieces (340g)
- ½ lb. scallops (227g)
- 1/3 lb. shrimp (150g)
- ¼ cup Italian parsley, fresh, chopped (113g)
- Lemon wedges

DIRECTIONS

1   Prep all the vegetables and fish. Heat oil in a skillet and sauté the leek, fennel, and garlic. Deglaze the pan with the white wine and place these ingredients in the soup maker. Add in the rest of the ingredients sans the lemon, parsley, and fish. Cook for 10 minutes. Then add in the fish and parsley and cook for another 15 minutes.

| 2 | Spoon into bowls, decorate with a lemon wedge, and serve right away. |

Nutritional Facts:

Calories: 425

Proteins: 33g

Carbs: 50g

Fats: 11g

VEGETARIAN SOUPS

CREAMY TWO MUSHROOM SOUP

Servings: 6

INGREDIENTS

- 1 ¼ lb. white mushrooms, chopped (567g)
- 1 tbsp. lemon juice, fresh
- 4½ cups vegetable stock (1L)
- 1 lb. shiitake mushrooms, chopped fine (454g)
- 2 lrg. cloves garlic, minced
- Salt and pepper to taste
- ¼ cupcrème fraiche (59mL)
- ½ tsp. ground coriander
- Parsley, fresh, chopped
- 2 tbsp. oil

DIRECTIONS

1 Add all the ingredients into the soup maker except the parsley and ¼ lb. white mushrooms. Cook on thick soup for 25 minutes. Then blend soup until creamy and smooth. Add in crème fraiche and mix thoroughly.

2 While cooking soup takes the extra mushrooms and in a skillet heat oil. Sauteed mushrooms in skillet and season with salt and pepper. Set aside.

3 Spoon the soup into bowls. Garnish with parsley and suited mushrooms. Serve.

Nutritional Facts:

Calories: 137

Proteins: 7g

Carbs: 10g

Fats: 0g

WHITE BEAN SOUP W/ CHARD

Servings: 6

INGREDIENTS

- 1 lb. Swiss chard (454g)
- 1 tbsp. olive oil
- 1 tbsp. garlic, minced
- 1 qt. vegetable broth (946mL)
- 2 cans cannellini beans, drained and rinsed
- ½ cup parmesan, grated(227g)
- Salt and pepper to taste

DIRECTIONS

1 Clean and prep all the fresh ingredients. Add all ingredients except the beans and parmesan into the soup maker. Cook for 20 minutes.

2 Then add in beans and cook for another 5 minutes. Mix in 1/2 cup parmesan cheddar and add salt and pepper to taste. Serve.

Nutritional Facts:

Calories: 196

Proteins: 17g

Carbs: 19g

Fats: 5.6g

MUSHROOM AND CARAMELIZED ONION SOUP

Servings: 6

INGREDIENTS

Soup:

- 1 tbsp. olive oil
- 8 cups onion, chopped (2kg)
- 5 cups shiitake mushroom tops, chopped (1kg)
- 4 cloves garlic, minced
- 2 thyme sprigs
- ½ cup dry white wine (118mL)
- 2 cans vegetable stock
- ½ tsp. salt
- ½ tsp. pepper

Toasts:

- 12 slices of French bread, toasted
- ¼ cup Gruyere, shredded (57g)
- ¼ cup Gorgonzola, crumbled (57g)
- ½ tsp. thyme, fresh, chopped

DIRECTIONS

1. Heat oil in a skillet over medium to high heat. Add onion to the dish; sauté 15 minutes, mixing as often as possible. Reduce the heat to medium-low; cook until dark (around 40 minutes), stirring occasionally. Add to the soup maker.

2. Place the rest of the ingredients for the soup into the soup maker and cook for 20 minutes.

3 While that is cooking you can make the toast. Organize bread in a solitary layer on a baking sheet. Top each slice with 1 tsp. Gruyere and 1 tsp. Gorgonzola. Cook for 2 minutes or until cheddar softens. Sprinkle thyme over cheddar.

4 Plate the soup and top each with 2 pieces of toast.

Nutritional Facts:

Calories: 208

Proteins: 8.9g

Carbs: 33.4g

Fats: 5.4g

SWEET POTATO SOUP CARIBBEAN-STYLE

Servings: 6

INGREDIENTS

- ◆ 2 tbsp. canola oil
- ◆ 2 sm. shallots, chopped
- ◆ 2 tbsp. lemongrass, chopped
- ◆ 1 tbsp. ginger, fresh, grated
- ◆ 5 cloves garlic, chopped
- ◆ 5½ cups vegetable stock (1L)
- ◆ 3½ lbs. sweet potatoes, cubed (1.5kg)
- ◆ 2½ tsps. salt
- ◆ ½ tsp. ground turmeric
- ◆ ¼ tsp. cayenne pepper
- ◆ 1 can coconut milk
- ◆ 3 tbsp. lime juice, fresh
- ◆ ¼ cup toasted almonds, sliced (57g)
- ◆ ¼ cup cilantro, fresh, chopped (57g)

DIRECTIONS

1 Prep and place all the ingredients except the coconut milk, lime juice, almond, and cilantro into the soup maker. Cook for 25 minutes. Skim coconut cream from the top of coconut milk; blend with 2 tbsp. of lime juice and set to the side.

2 Pour soup into a blender. Then whisk coconut milk in the can and 1 tablespoon lime juice in a medium-sized bowl until smooth and mix into soup. Blend until combined thoroughly. Empty soup into bowls, and sprinkle with coconut cream blend. Garnish with almonds and cilantro.

Nutritional Facts:

Calories: 205

Proteins: 4.5g

Carbs: 40g

Fats: 3.8g

CREAM OF ARUGULA

Servings: 6

INGREDIENTS

- 1 tbsp. olive oil
- 1 med. onion, chopped
- 2 cloves garlic, chopped
- 1 tsp. cornstarch
- 6 cups vegetable broth (1.5L)
- ½ cup milk (118mL)
- 10 oz. baby arugula (283g)
- ¼ cup mixed fresh herbs of your choice (57g)
- 4 tbsp. Greek yogurt
- 2 tbsp. chives, fresh, chopped

DIRECTIONS

1 Warm the olive oil in a skillet over a medium to low heat. Add the onion and garlic; cook until fragrant. Mix in cornstarch.

2 Place that mix and all ingredients except the Greek yogurt and chives into a soup maker. Cook on a thick soup setting for 25 minutes. Then blend soup until smooth.

3 Serve topped with Greek yogurt and chives.

Nutritional Facts:

Calories: 88

Proteins: 6g

Carbs: 8g

Fats: 3.9g

CREAM OF ARTICHOKE

Servings: 4

INGREDIENTS

- 2 tbsp. extra-virgin olive oil
- ½ cup shallots, chopped
- 3 cloves garlic, minced
- 3 cups vegetable stock
- 1 pkg. artichoke hearts, frozen
- 1 pkg. smooth tofu, drained
- 1 cup peas, frozen
- ¼ cup cream
- ¾ tsp. salt
- ½ tsp. pepper
- ¼ cup crème fraiche
- 2 tbsp. parsley, chopped

DIRECTIONS

1 Place all ingredients except cream, crème fraiche and parsley in the soup maker. Cook on the thick soup setting for 20 minutes. Then blend soup and mix in the cream.

2 Serve topped with crème fraiche and olive oil; garnish with parsley.

Nutritional Facts:

Calories: 285

Proteins: 13g

Carbs: 19g

Fats: 17g

GOLDEN BEET SOUP

Servings: 6

INGREDIENTS

- ½ tbsp. butter
- 1 lrg. fennel bulb, chopped
- 4 cloves garlic, chopped
- ½ tsp. salt
- ½ tsp. turmeric
- ¼ cup dry white wine (59mL)
- 2 lbs. golden beets, cubed
- 6 cups water (1.5L)
- ¾ cup red beet, julienned (170g)
- 2 tsps. lemon juice, fresh
- 1 tsp. sugar
- 3 tbsp. cilantro, fresh, chopped
- ¼ cup sesame seeds (57g)
- 1/8 tsp. cayenne pepper

DIRECTIONS

1 Melt the butter in a skillet and add the fennel, garlic, and salt; cook until tender and add to the soup maker. Add all ingredients except for the last five. Cook for 25 minutes.

2 While the soup is cooking, combine red beets, juice, sugar, and cilantro; let stand 30 minutes. Drain. Set aside

3   Warmth a huge cast-iron skillet over high and add in the sesame seeds. Toast until lightly browned and set to the side.

4   Blend the soup until smooth. Salt and pepper to taste. Serve topped with red beets and toasted sesame seeds.

Nutritional Facts:

Calories: 129

Proteins: 4g

Carbs: 21g

Fats: 3.8g

RED PEPPER & TOMATO GAZPACHO

Servings: 4

INGREDIENTS

- 2 bell peppers, red, chopped
- 5 lrg. tomatoes, chopped
- 2 cups cucumber, chopped (454g)
- ½ cup green onion, chopped(113g)
- 3 tbsp. extra-virgin olive oil
- 2 tbsp. white wine vinegar
- ½ tsp. salt
- ½ tsp. pepper
- 1 lrg. clove garlic, minced
- Mixed frozen vegetable medley
- Parsley, fresh, chopped

DIRECTIONS

1 Preheat the grill to high. Place peppers on the grill cut side down. Sear for 10 minutes or until peppers are darkened. Remove and wrap peppers with aluminum foil. Let stand 10 minutes; peel the skin off. Place in the soup maker.

2 Heat an enormous pan of water to boiling. Score the bottoms of the tomatoes in an X shape with the tip of a paring blade. Add to boiling water; let cook for 1 minute. Remove and place tomatoes into an ice bath. Let stand for 3 minutes. Remove skin from tomatoes and chop. Add the tomatoes, cucumber and rest of ingredients except the medley and parsley. Cook for 5 minutes and then blend.

3 Remove soup and chill for at least two hours. Then steam a vegetable medley and let sit as well. Serve cold topped with medley and garnished with parsley.

Nutritional Facts:

Calories: 103

Proteins: 3g

Carbs: 13g

Fats: 5.2g

ROASTED CARROT SOUP

Servings: 6

INGREDIENTS

- ¼ lb. carrots, chopped (113g)
- 1 tbsp. olive oil
- 1/8 tsp. salt
- 2 cups onion, chopped (454g)
- 2 tbsp. red curry paste
- 2 tsps. ginger, fresh, grated
- 1 tsp. red pepper flakes
- 1 can cannellini beans, drained
- 3 cups vegetable stock (709mL)
- 1 can coconut milk
- 3 tbsp. lime juice, fresh
- ½ tsp. pepper
- 1 cup cilantro, fresh. chopped (227g)
- 2 avocados, chopped
- 1 cup cooked lentils (227g)

DIRECTIONS:

1   Preheat the stove to 450°F (232°). Toss together carrots, 1/2 teaspoons oil, and 1/2 teaspoon salt on a large foil-lined baking sheet. Cook until carrots are tender, around 20 minutes.

2   Prep the rest of veggies and ingredients (except lime juice, cilantro, lentils, and avocado) and add to the soup maker. When carrots are done, add to the maker and cook for 25 minutes. While the soup is cooking, prepare lentils according to package instructions. When the soup is done, blend until smooth.

3 Season to taste and add lime juice. Then serve topped with cilantro, avocado, and lentils.

Nutritional Facts:

Calories: 363

Proteins: 11g

Carbs: 47g

Fats: 17g

ZESTY TOMATO SOUP

Servings: 4

INGREDIENTS

- 1 can whole tomatoes
- 1 jar cooked red peppers, drained
- ¼ cup cream (59mL)
- ½ tsp. salt
- 1 tsp. sugar
- ½ tsp. pepper
- 2 cloves garlic, chopped

DIRECTIONS

1 Add all ingredients into a soup maker and cook for 15 minutes. Then blend until smooth and serve.

Nutritional Facts:

Calories: 26
Proteins: 1g
Carbs: 5.2g
Fats: 0g

BONUS

LOW CARB RECIPES

GYRO SOUP

Servings: 6

INGREDIENTS

- 2 lbs. ground lamb (907g)
- 5 cups of water
- 1 can diced tomatoes, undrained
- 1 med. onion, chopped
- ¼ cup red wine
- 6 cloves garlic, minced
- 3 tbsp. mint, fresh, chopped
- 1 tbsp. dried marjoram
- 1 tbsp. dried rosemary
- 1½ tsp. salt
- ½ tsp. pepper
- Greek yogurt
- Feta, crumbled

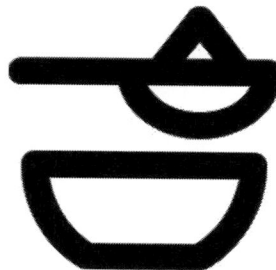

DIRECTIONS

1 In a skillet, cook lamb over medium-high heat browned. Add to the soup maker along with the rest of the ingredients sans the yogurt and feta. Cook on a thick soup setting for 25 minutes.

2 Serve topped with yogurt and garnished with feta.

Nutritional Facts:

Calories: 329

Proteins: 27g

Carbs: 7g

Fats: 20g

ROASTED SQUASH SOUP

Servings: 4

INGREDIENTS

- 1 lrg. butternut squash, cubed
- 2 potatoes, cubed
- 3 tbsp. extra-virgin olive oil
- Salt and pepper to taste
- 1 tbsp. margarine
- 1 onion, sliced
- 1 stalk celery, chopped fine
- 1 lrg. carrot, chopped
- 1 tbsp. thyme, fresh, chopped
- 1 qt. chicken stock (1L)

DIRECTIONS

1 Preheat the stove to 400°F (204°C). On a baking sheet, coat butternut squash and potatoes with 2 tablespoons of olive oil and season liberally with salt and pepper. Cook until delicate, 25 minutes.

2 Prep the rest of veggies and in a large skillet melt butter. Then sauté veggies until just tender. Add them, the squash and potatoes into the soup maker. Cook for 15 minutes.

3 Move mix to blender and process until smooth. Serve garnished with thyme.

Nutritional Facts:

Calories: 244

Proteins: 4.7g

Carbs: 41g

Fats: 7.7g

CAULIFLOWER CHOWDER W/ BACON

Servings: 6

INGREDIENTS

- 4 slices bacon, chopped
- 1 med. onion, chopped
- 2 med. carrots, chopped
- 2 stalks celery, chopped
- Salt and pepper to taste
- 2 cloves garlic, minced
- 2 tbsp. flour
- 2 sprigs thyme, chopped
- 1 head cauliflower, cut into florets
- 1 qt. vegetable stock (1L)
- 1 cup milk (237mL)

DIRECTIONS

1 In a skillet cook bacon until crisp. Move to a paper towel-lined plate.

2 In the same skillet heat oil and add in onion, carrots, and celery. Season and sauté until just tender. Then add in garlic cook until just fragrant. Include flour and cook for a few minutes. Move mixture to soup maker. Place the remaining ingredients except the milk into the maker and cook for 25 minutes.

3 Then heat milk and add soup to the warmed milk. Mix well. Season to taste and serve garnished with bacon crumbles.

Nutritional Facts:

Calories: 146

Proteins: 5g

Carbs: 13.7g

Fats: 8.3g

CREAMY LEEK & CAULIFLOWER SOUP

Servings: 4

INGREDIENTS

- 3 tbsp. extra-virgin olive oil
- 2 leeks, chopped
- 5 cloves garlic, minced
- 1 potato, chopped
- 1 lrg. head cauliflower, cut into florets
- Salt and pepper to taste
- 2 cups chicken broth(473mL)
- Chives, fresh, chopped
- Bacon

DIRECTIONS

1 In a large skillet over medium, heat olive oil. Add the leeks and cook until brilliant, 4 minutes. Include garlic and cook until fragrant.

2 Add all the ingredients except chives and bacon into a soup maker. Toss in the sautéed veggies and cook for 25 minutes.

3 Cook bacon and place it on a paper towel-lined plate. When the soup is cooked, move to the blender and process.

4 Season with salt and pepper to taste. Serve topped with bacon and garnished with chives.

Nutritional Facts:

Calories: 140

Proteins: 4.2g

Carbs: 21.4g

Fats: 5g

CHICKEN & MUSHROOM SOUP

Servings: 4

INGREDIENTS

- 2 tbsp. extra-virgin olive oil
- 1 lb. chicken breasts, skinless, boneless (454g)
- 1 lrg. onion, diced
- 2 cloves garlic, minced
- 1 lb. mushrooms, chopped (454g)
- 2 lrg. carrots, sliced
- 2 stalks celery, chopped
- Salt and pepper to taste
- 4 cups chicken stock (946mL)
- ¾ cup heavy cream (177mL)

DIRECTIONS

1 In a large skillet over medium to high, heat 1 tablespoon oil. Add chicken and cook until browned on each side. Move to a cutting board and cut into little pieces. Add to the soup maker.

2 Place all ingredients except the heavy cream on the soup maker. Cook for 25 minutes.

3 Season to taste and add in the cream. Mix well. Let cook for another 5 minutes. Then serve.

Nutritional Facts:

Calories: 634

Proteins: 42.3g

Carbs: 93.4g

Fats: 17g

TUSCAN CHICKEN SOUP

Servings: 6

INGREDIENTS

- 1 tbsp. extra-virgin olive oil
- ½ onion, chopped
- 2 celery stalks, chopped
- 3 cloves garlic, minced
- ½ tsp. red pepper flakes
- Salt and pepper to taste
- 6 cupschicken broth (1.5L)
- ½ lemon, juiced
- ¼ lb. chicken breast, skinless, boneless (113g)
- 1 can artichoke hearts, drained and quartered
- 1 cup mozzarella, shredded (227g)
- 1 cup parmesan, grated (227g)
- 4 cup baby spinach, chopped (907g)
- 2 tbsp. parsley, fresh, chopped

DIRECTIONS

1 In a skillet over medium warmth, heat oil. Include onion and celery and cook until delicate, 6 minutes. Include garlic and red pepper pieces if utilizing and cook until fragrant. Add to the soup maker.

2 In the same skillet heat more oil and add in the chicken. Cook until golden on both sides. Chop and add to the soup maker. Add in the rest of the ingredients except the spinach. Cook for 20 minutes.

3 Mix in spinach and let sit until spinach wilts. Serve with parsley and more parmesan.

Nutritional Facts:

Calories: 260

Proteins: 35.7g

Carbs: 12g

Fats: 7.5g

POZOLE

Servings: 6

INGREDIENTS

- 4 cup chicken stock (946mL)
- 3 chicken breast, boneless, skinless, cubed
- 2 poblano peppers, chopped
- 1 onion, chopped
- 2 cloves garlic, minced
- 1 tbsp. cumin
- 1 tbsp. oregano
- 2 tsp. chili powder
- 2 tsp. salt
- Pepper
- 2 cups hominy, drained (454g)
- Radishes, sliced thin
- Cabbage, sliced thin
- Cilantro, chopped

DIRECTIONS

1 In a skillet heat oil and season chicken. Add the chicken and sauté until browned.

2 Place all ingredients with the exception of hominy, radishes, cabbage, and cilantro into the soup maker. Cook on for 25 minutes.

3 Add in the hominy and cook for another 5 minutes.

4 Serve soup garnished with radish, cabbage, and cilantro.

Nutritional Facts:

Calories: 121

Proteins: 5.6g

Carbs: 21g

Fats: 2.3g

KETO DIET SOUP RECIPES

BUFFALO WINGZ SOUP

Servings: 8

INGREDIENTS

- 2 lbs. rotisserie chicken, shredded (907g)
- 3 tbsp. ranch seasoning
- 1 huge head cauliflower, chopped
- 5 cups chicken stock (1L)
- 1 cup water (237mL)
- 1 lb. carrots, chopped (454g)
- 6 stalks celery, chopped
- 1 med. onion, diced
- 1 tbsp. butter
- 1 cup buffalo sauce (237mL)
- Green onion, chopped
- Blue cheese, crumbled

DIRECTIONS

1. Sauté carrots, celery, and onion in a skillet with melted butter. Place is a soup maker. Add all the ingredients except for the green onion and blue cheese. Cook for 25 minutes.

2. Serve hot with green onion and blue cheddar as garnishes.

Nutritional Facts:

Calories: 364

Proteins: 31g

Carbs: 15g

Fats: 18g

TACO SOUP - CHICKEN

Servings: 8

INGREDIENTS

- 2 lb. chicken breasts, boneless, skinless(907g)
- 2 pkgs. cream cheese
- 1 pkt. ranch seasoning
- 3 tbsp. taco seasoning
- 2 can diced tomatoes and green chiles
- 4 cups chicken broth (946mL)

DIRECTIONS

1 In a large skillet, heat oil and cook chicken until browned on both sides. Chop or shred. Add to the soup maker. Top with remaining ingredients. Cook for 20 minutes.

2 Serve with cheese, cilantro, crushed tortilla chips, and sour cream

Nutritional Facts:

Calories: 549
Proteins: 56.6g
Carbs: 7.8g
Fats: 31.1g

GARLICKY CHICKEN SOUP

Servings: 4

INGREDIENTS

- 2 tbsp. butter
- 2 cups rotisserie chicken, shredded(226g)
- 4 oz. cream cheese (113g)
- 2 tbsp. garlic puree
- 14.5 oz chicken broth (411mL)
- ¼ cup heavy cream (59mL)
- Salt to taste

DIRECTIONS

1 Melt butter and toss the chicken in it. Add it into the soup maker. Include the rest of the ingredients except for the cream cheese and heavy cream. Cook for 15 minutes.

2 When the cream cheddar has softened add into the soup and mix until thoroughly combined. Then when the soup is done add in cream and mix well. Serve.

Nutritional Facts:

Calories: 307

Proteins: 18g

Carbs: 2g

Fats: 25g

ZOODLE & THAI CHICKEN SOUP

Servings: 8

INGREDIENTS

- 1 tbsp. coconut oil
- ¼ med. onion, chopped
- 1 jalapeño, chopped
- ½ tbsp. green curry paste
- 2 cloves garlic, minced
- 6 cups chicken broth (1.5L)
- 1 can coconut milk
- 1 med. red pepper, chopped fine
- 1 lb. chicken breasts, chopped small (454g)
- 2 tbsp. fish sauce
- ¼ cup cilantro, fresh, chopped (57g)
- 2 med. zucchini, spiralized
- 1 lime cut into wedges

DIRECTIONS

1 In a skillet heat coconut oil and when melted season the chicken with salt and pepper. Then sauté until browned.

2 In a large saucepan, heat the coconut oil until softened. Then add the onions and sauté until softened. Mix in the jalapeño, curry paste, and garlic, and sauté until fragrant. Include the chicken broth and coconut milk, mix until combined. Add all ingredients other than the lime, cilantro, and zoodles to the soup maker. Pour broth over ingredients. Cook for 25 minutes.

3 While the soup is cooking, spiralize your zucchini and place a portion in each bowl. Once the soup is done, add in the cilantro. Then serve the soup over the zoodles with a lime wedge.

Nutritional Facts:

Calories: 277

Proteins: 21.3g

Carbs: 6.6g

Fats: 16.1g

CREAMY ZUCCHINI SOUP

Servings: 4

INGREDIENTS

- ½ sm. onion, chopped
- 2 cloves garlic, minced
- 3 med. zucchini, chopped
- 32 oz. chicken broth (946mL)
- 2 tbsp. sour cream
- Salt and pepper to taste
- Parmesan, grated

DIRECTIONS

1 Combine chicken stock, onion, garlic, and zucchini in your soup maker. Cook for 25 minutes.

2 Remove from soup maker and to a blender. Purée along with the sour cream until smooth.

3 Taste for salt and pepper and adjust if needed. Serve hot garnished with parmesan.

Nutritional Facts:

Calories: 60

Proteins: 3.5g

Carbs: 10g

Fats: 1g

LIME CHICKEN AND AVOCADO SOUP

Servings: 6

INGREDIENTS

- ½ lb. chicken breasts, boneless, skinless (227g)
- 1 tbsp. olive oil
- 1 cup green onions, chopped(227g)
- 2 jalapeños, minced
- 2 cloves garlic, minced
- 14.5 oz chicken broth (428mL)
- 2 tomatoes, diced
- ½ tsp. ground cumin
- Salt and pepper to taste
- 1/3 cup cilantro, fresh, chopped(71g)
- 3 tbsp. lime juice, fresh
- 3 med. avocados, diced
- Tortilla chips
- Monterrey Jack
- Sour cream

DIRECTIONS

1 In a large skillet, heat olive oil over a medium heat. When hot, add in the green onions and jalapenos; sauté until delicate, around 2 minutes. Then add garlic and cook until fragrant. Add it into the soup maker. In the same skillet sauté the cut-up chicken until brown on all sides.

2 Include the chicken broth, tomatoes, cumin, season with salt and pepper to taste and the chicken. Cook for 20 minutes.

3 Then open the soup maker and mix in cilantro and lime juice.

4 Add avocados to soup just before serving. Serve topped with tortilla chips, cheddar, and sour cream.

Nutritional Facts:

Calories: 369

Proteins: 32g

Carbs: 15g

Fats: 21g

CREAMY ASPARAGUS SOUP

Servings: 4

INGREDIENTS

- 2 tbsp. butter
- 1 clove garlic, minced
- 2 lb. asparagus, cut into 1" pieces
- Salt and pepper to taste
- 2 cups chicken broth
- ½ cup heavy cream
- Chives, fresh, chopped
- Dill, fresh, chopped

DIRECTIONS

1   In a large saucepan heat the butter. Sauté garlic until it is fragrant, then add in the asparagus and season with salt and pepper. Cook for five minutes then add it to the soup maker. Add in the rest of the ingredients except for chives and dill. Cook in the soup maker for 20 minutes.

2   Move to blender and puree soup. Then add in the cream and mix well. Season with salt and pepper to taste.

3   Topping with more cream and garnish with chives and dill.

Nutritional Facts:

Calories: 168

Proteins: 7.8g

Carbs: 11g

Fats: 12.3g

DISCLAIMER

Printed in Great Britain
by Amazon

36127108R00066